"I won't give this to the genie," she said to herself, "because he said that the flower was all he wanted."

When the Princess had settled her unicorn into one of the stables, she returned to the cellar. The genie was nowhere to be seen, so she picked up the lamp and rubbed it once more with the hem of her dress. The genie appeared instantly and she gave him the magical flower.

"Thank you for fulfilling my first request," he said. "Now, I only need you to complete two more tasks for me and I will be freed from the lamp forever."

The Princess also longed to wish for a beautiful necklace, but she was a kind and generous girl and wanted to help the genie.

"What can I do for you?" she asked.

"I would like you to bring me a precious pure white pearl," he said. "It can only be found at the bottom of the Mystical Lake and that is all I want."

The Princess hated swimming and it was said that a giant serpent lived in the Mystical Lake, but she wanted to help the genie, so she made her way to the lake, took a deep breath and jumped into the cold, deep water. She swam down to the bottom and searched through the mud until she found the pure white pearl. She was about to swim back up when she spotted something red and shiny. At first, she was worried that it might be the eye of a serpent, but then she saw a golden clasp.

It was the most beautiful ruby necklace, which looked as if it had been lost for years. She scooped it up and reached the surface just before she ran out of breath. Gasping for air, she climbed out of the freezing water and hurried back to the castle, where she laid the beautiful ruby necklace on a velvet cushion in her bedroom.

The Enchanted Forest was dark and frightening and the Princess had heard that bears lived there but, nevertheless, she agreed, and set off to find the magical flower. The ground was wet underfoot and, before long, the Princess's shoes were soaked and the bottom of her dress was covered in mud.

"Oh dear, this task is a lot harder than I expected," the Princess said to herself, as she struggled through the tangled branches to the heart of the forest where the tallest tree stood. At last, she came upon the flower but, as she bent down to pick it, she heard something moving nearby. At first, she was worried that it might be a bear, but then she spotted a little horn poking through the leaves. Grasping the flower in one hand, the Princess peered into the bushes.

Nestled in the undergrowth was a baby unicorn. The Princess was thrilled. It was all alone, so she helped it to its feet and gently led it out of the forest, so she could care for it back at the castle.

"I won't give this to the genie," she said to herself, "because he said that the pearl was all he wanted."

As before, there was no sign of the genie in the cellar when she went back, so she rubbed the lamp again and he reappeared.

"Thank you fulfilling my second request," he said, as she gave him the pure white pearl. "Now, I have one final thing to ask of you."

The Princess would have liked to have used one wish for herself and wished for a handsome Prince to take her to the ball that evening, but she wanted the genie to be free.

"What can I do for you?" she asked.

"My last request is simple," the genie said. "All I ask for is a pink rose."

The Princess thought this would be easy and she hurried straight to the royal rose garden. But when she got there, she looked at the garden in dismay.

It was badly overgrown and every rose she could see was red. At last, she spotted a single pink flower, but it was right in the middle of the garden. As the Princess fought her way through the bushes, their thorns ripped her dress. She tried hard not to cry — she was cold and wet, her shoes were ruined and now her dress was not just covered in mud, it was torn, as well.

Yet, the Princess was determined to complete her final task, so she struggled through the bushes, picked the pink rose and returned with it to the cellar. She rubbed the lamp and the genie appeared.

"Thank you for fulfilling my third request," he said. "You have freed me forever!"

At that moment, the Princess was dazzled by a magical, sparkling light that encircled the genie and lit up the cellar's darkest corners. When she could see clearly again, the genie had disappeared and, in his place, stood a tall and handsome Prince.

"I was once cold-hearted and thought only of myself," the Prince explained. "To punish me for my selfish ways, a witch put a spell on me, trapping me in that lamp until I could find someone who was willing to complete three tasks for me out of the goodness of their heart. Now I would like to use the last of my magic to do something for you."

There was another flash of blinding light and, in an instant, the Princess' muddy, wet and torn dress was replaced by a beautiful ballgown. The Prince took her hand and asked if she would accompany him to the ball that evening.

All the Princess' wishes had been granted and, in time, the Prince and Princess were married. The unicorn was a guest at their wedding and the bride carried a bouquet of pink roses arranged around a magical mandragon flower. On her finger was a pure white pearl ring and she wore a beautiful ruby necklace.

Aladdin's Lamp

A long time ago, in faraway China, there lived a poor tailor, his wife and their son, Aladdin. The tailor worked hard and hoped that his son would one day enter the family business. But all Aladdin liked to do was spend time with his friends. Even when his father died, Aladdin didn't stop being lazy.
It was left to his poor old mother to bring a little money into the house by spinning cotton.

One day, while he was lazing around as usual, a stranger approached Aladdin and said, "My goodness, but you must be Aladdin. You look just like your father. I am your father's brother who has been away for many years. Please take me to your mother at once."
Aladdin was surprised. He didn't think he had an uncle, but did as he was told, anyway. When his mother saw the stranger she was also confused and said, "Yes, my husband did have a brother. I never met him. I thought he died many years ago." But it was such a happy meeting and the stranger seemed such a nice man, she found it easy to believe that he was her dead husband's brother.

What Aladdin and his mother didn't know was that the stranger was an evil magician who had picked Aladdin. He wanted to use Aladdin for his own ends and then get rid of him.

The magician told the boy he'd like to show him around the richer parts of the city. Suddenly, without warning, the magician stopped and pulled on a big metal ring attached to a flat stone in the middle of the street. Underneath the stone were stairs, leading down into darkness.

"Nephew," began the magician. "In the cave you will find a dirty old lamp. Empty the oil from it and bring it to me. The lamp is the only thing I wish for."

Aladdin was a little nervous, but the magician had given him a beautiful emerald ring to keep if he promised to bring the lamp back. Aladdin went slowly down the stairs. At the bottom, he found the three caves that were full of gold and silver.

There, he saw the old oil lamp. He picked it up, poured out the old, dirty oil and walked back until he reached the stairs again.

The magician was waiting for him at the top of the stairs.

"Give me the lamp," he said eagerly.

"Help me out of here first and then I'll give you the lamp," said Aladdin.

"I want it now!" cried the magician, and tried to grab the lamp out of Aladdin's hand. But as the two of them struggled, the stone suddenly fell back over the hole, shutting Aladdin, with the lamp, firmly inside.

The magician quickly realized that his plan had failed and left China, never to be seen again.

For two days, Aladdin stayed in the cave without any food, or water. He was getting very weak. Then, by chance, he rubbed the ring the magician had given him. All of a sudden, there was a blinding flash and a very large man appeared in front of him.

"Who are you?" asked Aladdin, in astonishment.

"I am the Genie of the Ring, master. Your wish is my command."

"Get me out of here!" cried Aladdin.

There was another blinding flash and Aladdin found himself standing in the alley above. He rushed home to his mother.

His mother cooked up whatever bits she had in the house, but it wasn't very much and, after he'd finished eating, Aladdin was still hungry.

"Maybe I can sell the lamp for food," he said. "I'd better give it a polish."

As soon as he started to rub the lamp, there was another blinding flash and another large man appeared.

Both Aladdin and his mother cried out in amazement.

"Who are you?" asked Aladdin, in a trembling voice.

"I am the Genie of the Lamp, master," said the large man. "Your wish is my command. What can I do for you?"

"Bring me a table full of food!" commanded Aladdin.

In the blink of an eye, a table appeared crammed full of the most delicious food, all served up on silver plates. When Aladdin and his mother had eaten everything, they sold the silver plates for a lot of money, which bought them enough food not to go hungry again for a very long time.

One day, while strolling in the market, Aladdin saw the Sultan's daughter, Princess Jasmine, and fell in love with her instantly. He went to see the Sultan and asked for his daughter's hand in marriage. As a gift, Aladdin gave the Sultan the stone-fruit he'd bought at the market.

But the Sultan's chief courtier wanted his son to marry the Princess, so he urged the Sultan to give Aladdin a test to prove himself. So the Sultan asked Aladdin for even more of the stone-fruit. But this time, the Sultan wanted forty servants to carry the fruit to his palace on forty silver platters.

When he was alone, Aladdin once again rubbed the lamp, and again the Genie appeared.

"What can I do for you, master?" he asked Aladdin.

"Send forty servants, bearing forty platters of stone-fruit, to the Sultan's palace," ordered Aladdin.

The Sultan was astonished when, the very next day, forty servants bearing forty platters of fruit arrived at his palace.

"Look at this!" exclaimed the Sultan. "I am now certain that Aladdin will make a fine husband for my daughter."

But the chief courtier suggested one final test for Aladdin.

"This is all well and good," he said. "But where would they live if they were married? If Aladdin is as wealthy as he says he is, he should be able to build a wonderful new palace for your daughter."

"You're right," said the Sultan, who was a simple man at heart and always thought that his chief courtier knew best. He told Aladdin that he could definitely marry his daughter if he built her a marvellous palace to live in. Aladdin summoned the Genie and once again, the Genie did his magic.

Shortly after, a brand new palace appeared right next door to where the Sultan lived. It was the finest palace anybody had ever seen. The walls were covered with gold and silver and every room was filled with fabulous treasures. Aladdin and the Princess had a huge wedding and lived a long and happy life. Aladdin never forgot the secret of his happiness and made sure to keep his lamp safe for the rest of his days.

The Enchanted Forest

Once upon a time, there was a Princess who lived in a grand palace with her father, the King, her stepmother, the Queen, and her two stepsisters. Although the Princess was always surrounded by servants, she was very lonely. She tried to make friends with her stepsisters, but they weren't always kind and never wanted to play with her. There weren't any other boys, or girls, in the palace, so there wasn't anyone else for the Princess to play with. The Princess spent a lot of time alone.

"I wish I had a best friend," thought the Princess sadly, as she walked through the palace gardens. She stopped to admire the beautiful roses, which grew beside the perfect lawns. The Princess wished she had someone to pick the pretty flowers for and to run with across the grass.

One day, the Princess heard her stepsisters laughing in the Queen's bedroom. They were dressing up in the Queen's finest clothes and trying on all her best jewels. The two sisters were smiling and joking, as they twirled across the floor wearing splendid ball gowns.

"Please can I dress up, too?" asked the Princess, eagerly.

Her stepsisters looked at her scornfully. "You're not big enough," the eldest sister said. "These clothes won't fit you," added her younger sister. "Why don't you go and play outside instead?"

"But I'd really like to stay here, with you," the Princess pleaded. She couldn't bear to spend another day on her own.

"You can't," said the younger sister, putting on a sparkling tiara and admiring her reflection in the mirror.

"Go away and leave us alone," said the older sister, turning her back on the Princess. The Princess went downstairs and into the gardens. A tear ran down her cheek as she started to explore the path that led into the woodlands. The leaves on the trees rustled and whispered invitingly as she wandered farther and farther into the forest.

The Princess walked until she saw a clearing ahead, where sunlight was streaming through the trees. She ran toward it and gasped in amazement. Standing in front of her was a beautiful unicorn. The unicorn pawed at the ground with a graceful leg as the sun's rays glistened on its golden horn. It stared at the Princess and she hesitated. She knew unicorns were very shy and she didn't want to startle it.

"Hello," said the Princess softly. "You're the most beautiful creature I've ever seen." The unicorn tossed its head and trotted over. It lowered its nose and allowed the Princess to gently stroke its silky coat.

"Unicorn, will you be my friend?" the Princess asked. The unicorn nuzzled its head into the Princess's arm.

The Princess was happier than she'd ever been. She sat down on the ground next to the unicorn and told it how lonely she was, how her stepsisters wouldn't let her play with them and how she longed for a friend. Although the unicorn didn't speak, the Princess could tell it was listening carefully.

When the Princess had finished talking, the unicorn trotted over to the side of the clearing and looked back at the Princess.

"Do you want me to follow you?" the Princess asked.

The unicorn nodded and the Princess followed it through the forest. Soon, the trees thinned and there was silver grass beneath their feet. The Princess gazed around. She was surrounded by vibrant red, purple and turquoise trees and a rainbow stream flowed nearby. There were beautiful flowers and the sky was pink with fluffy blue clouds drifting across it. The Princess couldn't believe her eyes. It was all so unusual and was totally different to anything she'd ever seen before. The unicorn had led her into an enchanted land.

"Where are we?" the Princess asked. The unicorn stopped walking and stamped its foot three times. Before she knew what was happening, the Princess was surrounded by friendly faces. She gasped as she saw fairies fluttering around her.

"Hello," one of the fairies said, in a voice that sounded like musical notes. "Who are you?"

"I'm a Princess from the kingdom on the other side of the forest," the Princess replied.

"A Princess," the fairies gasped with glee, clapping their hands together. They flew around excitedly. "We've never met a real Princess before."

"I've never met a real fairy before, either," the Princess said shyly. "Or a unicorn, for that matter."

"Stay with us for a while," one of the fairies begged. "We'd love to play with you. We hope you'll be our friend."

"You'd like to be my friend?" the Princess asked.

"Of course," the fairies replied.

The Princess had a wonderful time. The fairies showed the Princess around the enchanted land. Then she played hide-and-seek with them, which the fairies won easily, because it's very difficult to find a fairy when she's hiding. After that, the Princess ate delicious tiny buttercup muffins and wild cherry tarts. She'd never had so much fun.

At the end of the afternoon, the purple sun began to set in the sky.

"I'd better go," the Princess said, sadly.

"You'll come back though, won't you?" one of the fairies asked. "We've had such a lovely time with you."

"Of course I will," the Princess replied, smiling happily. "I'm lucky to have made so many wonderful new friends. I'll see you tomorrow."

The fairies waved goodbye as the Princess walked back through the trees. When she got home, her stepsisters were waiting and they said they were sorry for not letting her join in. The girls became good friends and the Princess introduced them to the fairies in the enchanted land. They all played happily together and, from that day on, the Princess was never lonely again.